Simple Checkmates

A.J. Gillam

Ballantine Books • New York

Special thanks to Ballantine's guest chess editor
Asuka Nakamura

Originally published in Great Britain in 1978 by B.T. Batsford
Limited, London.

NSCF   is the official logo of the National Scholastic Chess Foundation. The NSCF logo was designed by Iromie Weeramantry.

http://www.randomhouse.com

Library of Congress Catalog Card Number: 95-96126

ISBN: 0-345-40307-X

Manufactured in the United States of America

First American Edition: May 1996

10   9   8   7   6

A NOTE TO PARENTS AND COACHES

How many times has a novice chess player reduced an opponent's forces to a lone king yet failed to checkmate? And how many times has a more experienced player failed to win a game by not seeing a simple checkmating sequence? Too many. Learning to execute a checkmate correctly is the first milestone in a chess player's development. Without checkmate, there is no victory.

Simple Checkmates by A. J. Gillam is one book that will successfully guide the reader through this early stage. It is an instructional book that contains a collection of positions where one player is about to checkmate the other. There are 433 in all—116 one-move checkmates and 317 of the two-move variety. The problems increase in complexity within each group of examples, progressing from relatively uncluttered positions that contain only a few pieces to more crowded positions where more options have to be considered. Nevertheless, no checkmate runs more than two moves deep. The author, a former school teacher who for many years coached the chess team at his local primary school in Nottingham, England, has established a framework to which he faithfully adheres. His message is practical: master basic checkmates before tackling longer sequences.

An attentive player will not have much difficulty in solving most of the one-move checkmates. It is simply a matter of scanning the entire chessboard and determining which pieces can deliver check. One of those checks has to be checkmate. However, checkmates that involve pins, discovered checks, or double checks are definitely harder to visualize. One of the strengths of *Simple Checkmates* is that the author anticipates such difficulties and offers valuable advice at the appropriate time.

Indeed, the author's main concern throughout *Simple Checkmates* is to ensure that the reader understand the process involved in solving these positions. In his introduction to the second half of the book, which deals with two-move checkmates, he explains the concept of move sequences, where consecutive moves are closely linked and can trigger a definite reaction. This is essential to understanding the flow of a game. Two-move checkmates constitute an easy introduction to this concept. There is a definite end to the sequence. The first move sets up the second, and the sequence ends in checkmate.

The clarity with which the material is presented and the logic with which it is arranged attest to Mr. Gillam's background as an educator. The most striking feature of *Simple Checkmates* may well be the author's emphasis on pattern recognition as a technique in solving problems. This is addressed in two ways. In the first place, the author provides a series of diagrams depicting typical checkmates that are carried out by each one of the pieces. The student is urged to study these patterns and to search for them while working through each position presented. Secondly, the positions themselves are grouped according to themes such as "Checkmates Using a Pin" or "Back Row Mates in Two Moves" so that a particular motif is stressed over and over again. It has often been suggested that chess masters store thousands of patterns in their minds and that their skill in charting the right course can be attributed to identifying these patterns within more complex positions. The student who assimilates the various patterns here will undoubtedly see a marked increase in his/her confidence in closing out a game.

The answers in *Simple Checkmates* are given in algebraic notation, which is well explained in the introductory pages. This form of notation is widely used today and is easy to comprehend as each square on the chessboard has only one designation. As Executive Director of the National Scholastic Chess Foundation (NSCF), I oversee the instruction of some 3,000 students on a weekly basis. All instructors within the NSCF use algebraic notation in the classroom. In my experience, any student who is old enough to learn the alphabet is quite capable of learning this new language with ease.

While *Simple Checkmates* is intended for chess players of all ages, the manner in which its material is arranged makes it particularly well suited for young players. The answers are provided on the same page underneath the diagram. This obviates the need to flip back and forth continuously between pages. The student now has the option of using the answers in the most advantageous way, either covering up the answer until the solution has been found or studying the diagram briefly before verifying the answer.

This new edition of *Simple Checkmates* contains several technical improvements that make the book easier to read. The diagrams have been enlarged and only two are presented on each page. Moreover, the use of the internationally acclaimed Linares font has made the diagrams clearer. All these changes, along with the increased type size, are designed to make the reader feel more comfortable if he/she chooses to tackle these checkmate exercises without setting up a chessboard.

I have always endorsed the philosophy that the player should become proficient in the rudiments of chess before venturing into more complex situations. I am delighted to find that *Simple Checkmates* supports this view. Finding material that is appropriate for beginning levels of play and does not introduce unnecessary complications is difficult. I am pleased to say that my task, and that every other chess coach, has been rendered much simpler now that *Simple Checkmates* is readily available.

—Sunil Weeramantry
Executive Director
National Scholastic Chess Foundation

Chairman, Chess in Education
U.S. Chess Federation

January 1996

INTRODUCTION

On pages 2 to 7 of this book you will find some of the most common checkmate positions found in chess. If you have only just learned the moves then these positions will be of great value to you and you should look at them carefully and make sure that you understand the idea of checkmate.

If you have just learned to play chess then answer these questions:

1: Do you know and understand what *en passant* is?

2: Do you know the rules of pawn promotion?

3: Do you know the rules of castling?

If the answer to any of these questions is *yes* then you are ready to read *Simple Checkmates*. If not, you need to read a book explaining how the pieces move.

In every position in this book, White plays up the board and it is White to move. In diagrams 1 to 116 White can checkmate in one move. In all the diagrams after number 116 White can checkmate in two moves.

The headings to the pages give you some idea of what to look for on each page. Diagrams 1 to 24 are very simple checkmates. Numbers 25–32 are checkmates by promoting a pawn and numbers 33 to 48 use a pin to checkmate Black. Pins are explained on page 9. Diagrams 49–96 are a mixture of all sorts of checkmates.

First try to work out the answers on your own. If you cannot do it then do not worry, just look up the answer and work it out from that. The important thing is that you understand the answer. In order to be able to work out the answers for yourself and quickly, you need practice. That is why there are so many examples in this book, even though some of them are quite similar to one another. By splitting the examples up into types we have tried to make it easier.

ROOK CHECKMATES

QUEEN CHECKMATES

BISHOP CHECKMATES

KNIGHT CHECKMATES

KNIGHT CHECKMATES

PAWN CHECKMATES

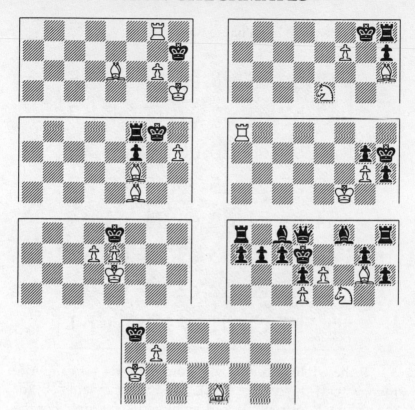

GIVING MOVES A NAME

Every square has a name like this:

a8	b8	c8	d8	e8	f8	g8	h8
a7	b7	c7	d7	e7	f7	g7	h7
a6	b6	c6	d6	e6	f6	g6	h6
a5	b5	c5	d5	e5	f5	g5	h5
a4	b4	c4	d4	e4	f4	g4	h4
a3	b3	c3	d3	e3	f3	g3	h3
a2	b2	c2	d2	e2	f2	g2	h2
a1	b1	c1	d1	e1	f1	g1	h1

If the white queen moves from d1 to d4 we can write this as Qd1-d4 or just Qd4. We use the letter B for the bishop, R for rook, N for knight and K for king. For the pawns we do not use a letter so if you see the move e4, it means that a pawn has moved to square e4.

When writing the moves of a game we put in the move numbers as well: 1 e4 e5 2 Nf3 Nc6. This means that on move one White played pawn to e4 and Black replied with pawn to e5. On move two White played knight to f3 and Black played knight to c6.

A capture is written with an 'x'. So Rxf3 means that a rook takes whatever is on f3.

Pawn captures are written by giving the file from which the pawn starts and the square where it finishes e.g. exd4 means a pawn on the e-file takes on d4.

PINS

A pin is a very simple idea. Look at diagram A below. The black bishop stands between the white rook and the black king. By the rules of chess, Black is not allowed to play a move which will put his own king in check. Therefore he is not allowed to move his bishop as any move by the bishop would leave the black king in check from the white rook. The bishop is said to be pinned.

It is important to notice that, even though the bishop is pinned, the white king cannot move to h3 as that square is attacked by the bishop and White would be moving into check himself.

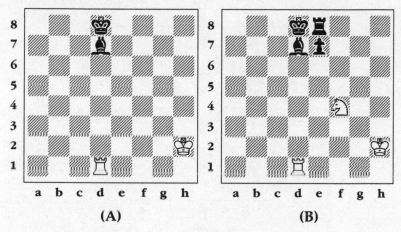

(A)   (B)

Look at diagram B. The bishop is still pinned and so White can play Ne6+ without fear of the knight being taken. Black's only move to get out of the check is Kc8. Now put a black piece on c8 in diagram B (a queen, rook or knight) and Ne6 will be checkmate!

In diagrams 33 to 48, White checkmates because a black piece is pinned and is therefore not allowed to capture the checkmating white piece.

CHECKMATE IN ONE MOVE

(1)

(2)

Answers

1: Re8 mate

2: Ra8 mate

CHECKMATE IN ONE MOVE

(3)

(4)

Answers

3: Rg8 mate

4: Qxg7 mate

CHECKMATE IN ONE MOVE

(5)

(6)

Answers

5: Nf7 mate

6: Bg7 mate

CHECKMATE IN ONE MOVE

(7)

(8)

Answers

7: b7 mate

8: Rxb8 mate

CHECKMATE IN ONE MOVE

(9)

(10)

Answers

9: Rd4 mate

10: Nh6 mate

CHECKMATE IN ONE MOVE

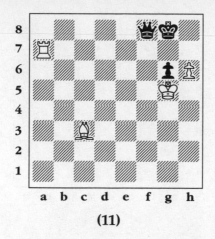

(11)

(12)

Answers

11: h7 mate

12: Be5 mate

CHECKMATE IN ONE MOVE

(13)

(14)

Answers

13: Qf7 mate

14: Qc8 mate

CHECKMATE IN ONE MOVE

(15)

(16)

Answers

15: Qc6 mate

16: Qh7 mate

CHECKMATE IN ONE MOVE

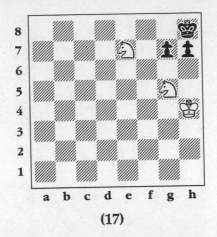

(17)

(18)

Answers

17: Nf7 mate

18: Qf7 mate or Qe8 mate

CHECKMATE IN ONE MOVE

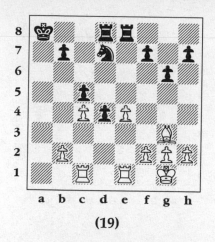

(19)

(20)

Answers

19: Ra1 mate

20: Rf7 mate

19

CHECKMATE IN ONE MOVE

(21)

(22)

Answers

21: Qe7 mate

22: Ra8 mate

CHECKMATE IN ONE MOVE

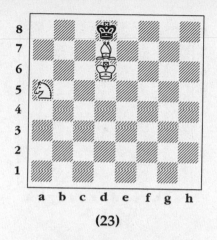

(23)

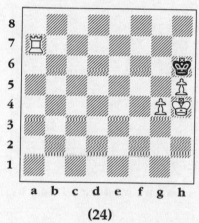

(24)

Answers

23: Nb7 or Nc6 mate

24: g5 mate

CHECKMATE BY PAWN PROMOTION

(25)

(26)

Answers

25: c8Q mate

26: c8N mate

CHECKMATE BY PAWN PROMOTION

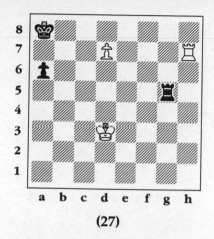

(27)

(28)

Answers

27: d8Q or d8R mate

28: g8Q or g8R mate

CHECKMATE BY PAWN PROMOTION

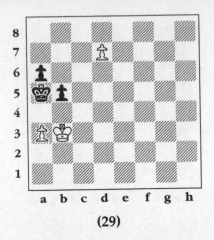

(29)

(30)

Answers

29: d8Q or d8B mate

30: c8N mate (if cxb8Q+ Black plays Kxb8)

24

CHECKMATE BY PAWN PROMOTION

(31)

(32)

Answers

31: b8Q mate

32: dxe8Q mate

CHECKMATE USING A PIN

(33)

(34)

Answers

33: Ng6 mate

34: d6 mate

CHECKMATE USING A PIN

(35)

(36)

Answers

35: Qxh7 mate

36: Rxe6 mate

CHECKMATE USING A PIN

(37)

(38)

Answers

37: Rxd6 mate

38: Nb6 or Nc7 mate

28

CHECKMATE USING A PIN

(39)

(40)

Answers

39: Rd8 mate

40: Nxf7 mate

29

CHECKMATE USING A PIN

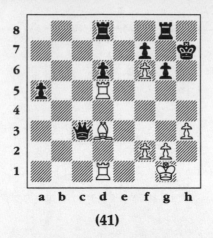

(41)

(42)

Answers

41: Rh5 mate

42: Rd4 mate

30

CHECKMATE USING A PIN

(43)

(44)

Answers

43: Qa6 mate

44: Re8 mate

CHECKMATE USING A PIN

(45)

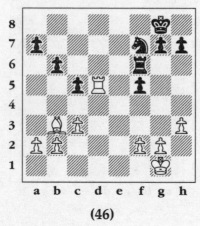

(46)

Answers

45: Rxa6 mate

46: Rd8 mate

32

CHECKMATE USING A PIN

(47)

(48)

Answers

47: Ng6 mate or Rxf7 mate

48: Ne6 mate

VARIOUS CHECKMATES IN ONE MOVE

(49)

(50)

Answers

49: Qe5 mate

50: Rxh7 mate

VARIOUS CHECKMATES IN ONE MOVE

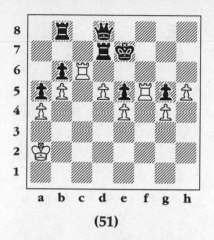

(51)

(52)

Answers

51: Re6 mate

52: Bh7 mate

VARIOUS CHECKMATES IN ONE MOVE

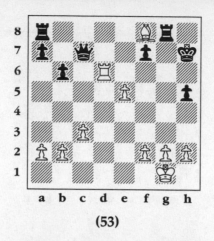

(53)

(54)

Answers

53: Rh6 mate

54: Bf7 mate

VARIOUS CHECKMATES IN ONE MOVE

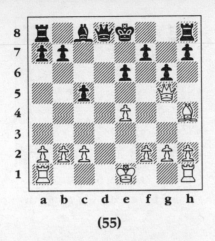

(55)

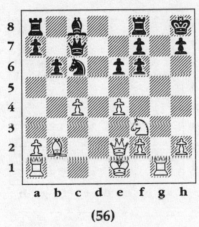

(56)

Answers

55: Qxd8 mate

56: Bxf6 mate

VARIOUS CHECKMATES IN ONE MOVE

(57)

(58)

Answers

57: Qh5 mate

58: Nf7 mate

VARIOUS CHECKMATES IN ONE MOVE

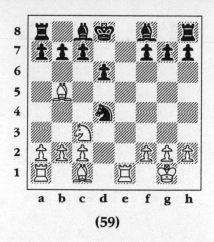

(59)

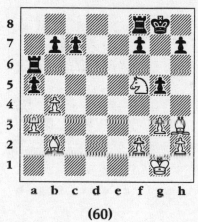

(60)

Answers

59: Re8 mate

60: Ne7 mate

VARIOUS CHECKMATES IN ONE MOVE

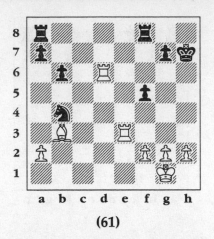

(61)

(62)

Answers

61: Rh3 mate

62: g3 mate

VARIOUS CHECKMATES IN ONE MOVE

(63)

(64)

Answers

63: Bh6 mate

64: Ba6 mate

VARIOUS CHECKMATES IN ONE MOVE

(65)

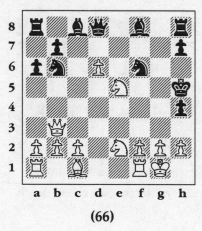

(66)

Answers

65: Nf4 mate

66: Qf7 mate

VARIOUS CHECKMATES IN ONE MOVE

(67)

(68)

Answers

67: Qh3 mate

68: Ng3 mate

VARIOUS CHECKMATES IN ONE MOVE

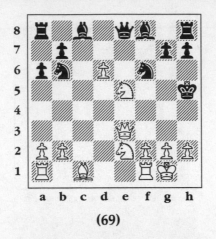

(69)

(70)

Answers

69: Qg5 mate

70: Ng3 mate

VARIOUS CHECKMATES IN ONE MOVE

(71)

(72)

Answers

71: g4 mate

72: Qg4 mate

VARIOUS CHECKMATES IN ONE MOVE

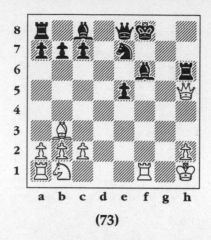

(73)

(74)

Answers

73: Qxh6 mate

74: Bf6 mate

VARIOUS CHECKMATES IN ONE MOVE

(75)

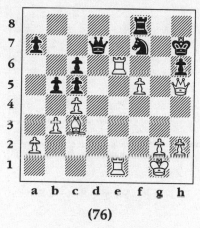

(76)

Answers

75: Ra3 mate

76: Qg6 mate

VARIOUS CHECKMATES IN ONE MOVE

(77)

(78)

Answers

77: Qxh7 mate

78: Ng6 mate

VARIOUS CHECKMATES IN ONE MOVE

(79)

(80)

Answers

79: Bg6 mate

80: Re8 mate

VARIOUS CHECKMATES IN ONE MOVE

(81)

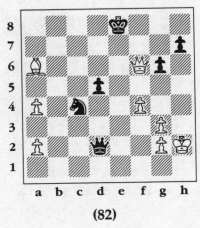

(82)

Answers

81: Ng7 mate

82: Bb5 mate

VARIOUS CHECKMATES IN ONE MOVE

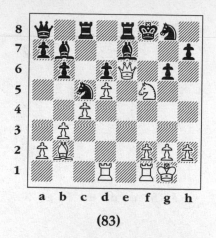

(83)

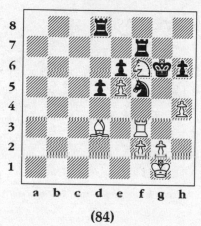

(84)

Answers

83: Bg7 mate

84: Rg3 mate

VARIOUS CHECKMATES IN ONE MOVE

(85)

(86)

Answers

85: Rh3 mate

86: Rg1 mate or Rg3 mate

VARIOUS CHECKMATES IN ONE MOVE

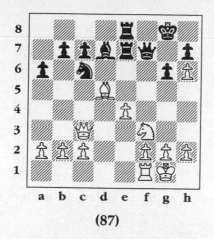

(87)

(88)

Answers

87: Qg7 mate

88: Nxg6 mate

VARIOUS CHECKMATES IN ONE MOVE

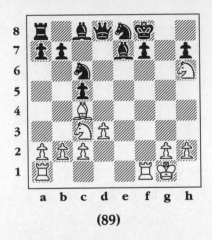

(89)

(90)

Answers

89: Rxf7 mate

90: Rxh8 mate

VARIOUS CHECKMATES IN ONE MOVE

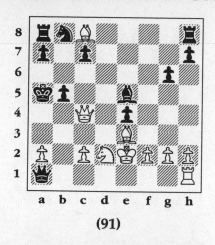

(91)

(92)

Answers

91: Nb3 mate

92: Re8 mate

VARIOUS CHECKMATES IN ONE MOVE

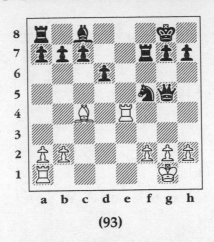

(93)

(94)

Answers

93: Re8 mate

94: Bxg4 mate

VARIOUS CHECKMATES IN ONE MOVE

(95)

(96)

Answers

95: Bxg7 mate

96: Bxg6 mate

DISCOVERED AND DOUBLE CHECKS

Discovered checks are quite common and it is therefore important for all players to be familiar with them. The idea is quite simple. In diagram C White is going to check the enemy king by moving his rook. No matter where the rook goes, the black king will be in check from the white bishop. This is a discovered check—one where the piece giving the check is not the piece that makes the move.

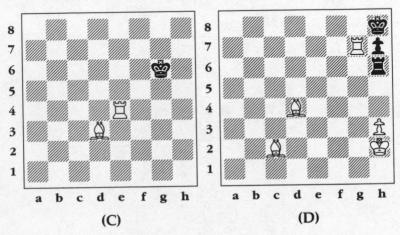

(C)   (D)

A double check is a special type of discovered check and is one of the most powerful moves in chess. If, in diagram C, the rook moves to g4 or e6 then Black will be in check twice, from the bishop by discovered check and from the rook by an ordinary check. The important thing about double checks is that you can only get out of them by moving your king. It is impossible to block both checks in one move and you cannot take both checking pieces in one move, so a king move is the only escape left. In moving out of double check the king can sometimes take one of the checking pieces, as in diagram D above.

In diagram D White can play a double check by moving his rook to g8 or by taking on h7. If Rg8+ then Black can reply Kxg8 but if Rxh7+ then both Kxh7 and Rxh7 leave the black king in check and so are illegal, so only Kg8 is possible.

Positions 97 to 116 all show checkmates in one move by discovered or double checks. These are more difficult than the earlier positions and need to be looked at carefully.

MATES BY DISCOVERED AND DOUBLE CHECK

(97)

(98)

Answers

97: Ng5 mate

98: Rd8 mate

MATES BY DISCOVERED AND DOUBLE CHECK

(99)

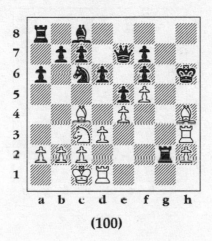

(100)

Answers

99: f7 mate

100: Bxf6 mate

MATES BY DISCOVERED AND DOUBLE CHECK

(101)

(102)

Answers

101: Bf8 mate

102: Rf8 or Rg6 mate

MATES BY DISCOVERED AND DOUBLE CHECK

(103)

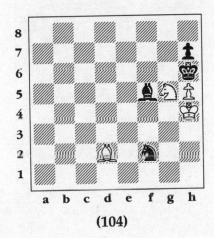

(104)

Answers

103: Nxg3 mate

104: Ne6 mate

MATES BY DISCOVERED AND DOUBLE CHECK

(105)

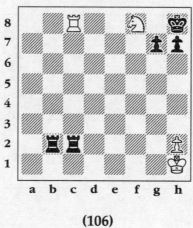

(106)

Answers

105: Be5 mate

106: Ng6 mate

MATES BY DISCOVERED AND DOUBLE CHECK

(107)

(108)

Answers

107: g8N mate

108: Ba5 mate

MATES BY DISCOVERED AND DOUBLE CHECK

(109)

(110)

Answers

109: Bg5 mate

110: dxe7 mate

MATES BY DISCOVERED AND DOUBLE CHECK

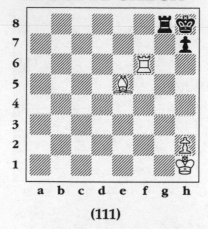

(111)

(112)

Answers

111: Rf8 mate

112: Rh6 mate

MATES BY DISCOVERED AND
DOUBLE CHECK

(113)

(114)

Answers

113: g8Q or g8R mate

114: Bd7 mate

MATES BY DISCOVERED AND DOUBLE CHECK

(115)

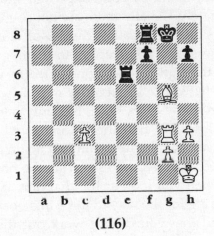

(116)

Answers

115: hxg8Q or hxg8R mate

116: Bf6 mate

CHECKMATE IN TWO MOVES

The rest of the diagrams in this book are all examples of White to play and checkmate in two moves. This means that after White's first move, no matter what Black plays, White can checkmate on his second move. This sounds difficult but it is the main purpose of this book to help you to learn to calculate such 'combinations', and one or two tips should help you considerably.

If you wish to play a move so that it will be easy for you to calculate your opponent's reply and, after that, your own next move, then you should look for a check. A check is the strongest type of move available on the chessboard as, by the rules of chess, your opponent must get out of check immediately. Usually there are not so many ways for him to do this and so it makes the job of working out his possible answers, and your replies to them, much simpler. As you work through the positions in the rest of this book you will find that White's first move in nearly all of them is a check and in many cases Black has only one possible reply. You will also find that there are a number of similar ideas which keep coming up again and again in these positions and you should begin to see what the final position is going to be when you look at the diagram. After this you can begin looking for the way to force this position.

If you find that you cannot work out the checkmate, then look at just the first move of the answer and work out the rest of the moves after that. If you don't want to try to work them out yourself, you will still learn a lot from working out the answer on the diagram and making sure that you understand how the checkmate comes about.

The most common type of checkmate found in beginners' games (and in the games of quite experienced players also) is the back row mate. The idea is very simple and you will find a number of back row mates shown in the sample checkmate positions at the beginning of the book. Look carefully at positions 1-3, 8, 14 and others. In all of them the black king is trapped against the back edge of the board and is checkmated along the back rank by a rook or queen. The same idea is often seen with the king trapped against the side of the board and checkmated along the a-file or h-file.

Because this type of checkmate is so common we have given a lot of examples. Positions 117-224 are all of the back row mate type although many of them have the black king trapped against the edge of the board instead of at the back.

In some of the positions there is more than one way to checkmate in two moves. Sometimes the other way is an unimportant one with only a slight difference in position but sometimes there will be a completely different checkmate.

In many of the positions White can win in other ways and even checkmate in three or four moves. However, we are interested only in finding the shortest possible checkmate as this is the one that gives Black the least chance of escaping. So look for the mate in two moves!

BACK ROW MATES IN TWO MOVES

(117)

(118)

Answers

117: 1 Re8+ Rxe8 2 Rxe8 mate

118: 1 Qe8+ Bxe8 2 Rxe8 mate

BACK ROW MATES IN TWO MOVES

(119)

(120)

Answers

119: 1 Rf8+ Rxf8 2 Qxf8 mate

120: 1 Rxe8+ Rxe8 2 Rxe8 mate

BACK ROW MATES IN TWO MOVES

(121)

(122)

Answers

121: 1 Qxf8+ Rxf8 2 Rxf8 mate or 1 Rxf8+ Rxf8 2 Qxf8 mate

122: 1 Qe8+ Rxe8 2 Rxe8 mate not 1 Rxd8+? Qxd8!

BACK ROW MATES IN TWO MOVES

(123)

(124)

Answers

123: 1 Qg8+ Rxg8 2 hxg8Q or hxg8R mate (double check!)

124: 1 Qxe8+ Rxe8 2 Rxe8 mate

BACK ROW MATES IN TWO MOVES

(125)

(126)

Answers

125: 1 Bxd4+ Rxd4 2 Rf8 mate

126: 1 Re8+ Bf8 2 either Rxf8 mate

BACK ROW MATES IN TWO MOVES

(127)

(128)

Answers

127: 1 Ra8+ Bxa8 2 Qc8 mate

128: 1 Rd8+ Bf8 2 Rxf8 mate

BACK ROW MATES IN TWO MOVES

(129)

(130)

Answers

129: 1 Rb7+ followed by Ra8 mate

130: 1 Rxe8+ Rxe8 2 Rxe8 mate

BACK ROW MATES IN TWO MOVES

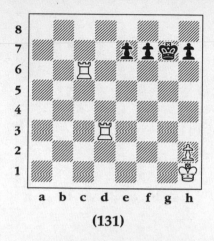

(131)

(132)

Answers

131: 1 Rg3+ followed by Rc8 mate

132: 1 Be4+ followed by Rd8 mate

BACK ROW MATES IN TWO MOVES

(133)

(134)

Answers

133: 1 f6+ followed by Rd8 mate

134: 1 e6+ followed by h8Q or h8R mate

BACK ROW MATES IN TWO MOVES

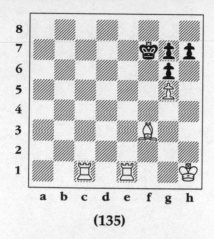

(135)

(136)

Answers

135: 1 Bd5+ Kf8 2 Rc8 mate

136: 1 Ng5+ Kg8 or Kh8 2 Rc8 mate

BACK ROW MATES IN TWO MOVES

(137)

(138)

Answers

137: 1 Nxd6+ or Nf6+ (double checks!) followed by
Re8 mate

138: 1 Rc8+ Rxc8 2 Qxc8 mate

BACK ROW MATES IN TWO MOVES

(139)

(140)

Answers

139: 1 Bh5+ Kf8 or Kg8 2 Re8 mate

140: 1 Qxf8+ (1Qc4+? Rd5!) Kxf8 2 Rb8 mate (2 Rd8+??
Rxd8) or 1 Rg7+ Kh8 2 Qxf8 mate

BACK ROW MATES IN TWO MOVES

(141)

(142)

Answers

141: 1 Bd5+ Kh8 2 Rf8 mate

142: 1 Bf6+ Kg8 2 Rh8 mate

84

BACK ROW MATES IN TWO MOVES

(143)

(144)

Answers

143: 1 Bd5+ Kh8 or Kh7 2 Rh1 mate

144: 1 Rh8+! Kxh8 2 Rf8 mate. It is easy to stalemate Black in this position. 1 Rhg1! or Kh2 or Kh3 all force the same mate.

BACK ROW MATES IN TWO MOVES

(145)

(146)

Answers

145: 1 g6+ Kg8 or Kh8 2 Re8 mate

146: 1 Bg5+ Kf8 2 Re8 mate

BACK ROW MATES IN TWO MOVES

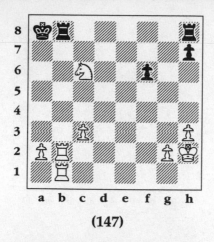

(147)

(148)

Answers

147: 1 Rxb8+ Rxb8 2 Rxb8 mate

148: 1 Nb7+ Ke8 2 Rc8 mate

BACK ROW MATES IN TWO MOVES

(149)

(150)

Answers

149: 1 Ng6+ hxg6 2 Rh1 mate

150: 1 Rxh7+ Kxh7 2 Rh1 mate

BACK ROW MATES IN TWO MOVES

(151)

(152)

Answers

151: 1 Be6+ Kh8 2 Rxf8 mate

152: 1 Qd8+! Kxd8 2 Rf8 mate

BACK ROW MATES IN TWO MOVES

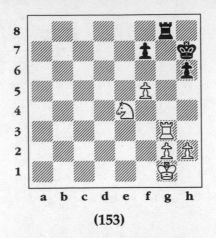

(153)

(154)

Answers

153: 1 Nf6+ Kh8 2 Rxg8 mate

154: 1 Qh7+ Rxh7 2 Rxh7 mate

BACK ROW MATES IN TWO MOVES

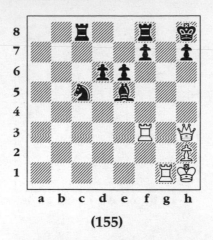

(155)

(156)

Answers

155: 1 Qxh7+ Kxh7 2 Rh3 mate

156: 1 Rh3+ Kg8 2 Rh8 mate

BACK ROW MATES IN TWO MOVES

(157)

(158)

Answers

157: 1 Qf8+ Rxf8 2 Rxf8 mate

158: 1 Qxh7+ Kxh7 2 Rh5 mate

BACK ROW MATES IN TWO MOVES

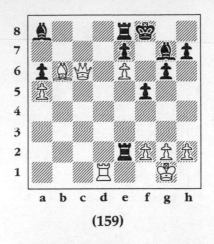

(159)

(160)

Answers

159: 1 Qxe8+ Kxe8 2 Rd8 mate

160: 1 Qc8+ Bxc8 2 Rxc8 mate or 1 Qc8+ Be8 2 Qxe8 mate

BACK ROW MATES IN TWO MOVES

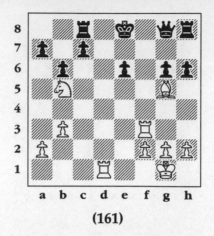

(161)

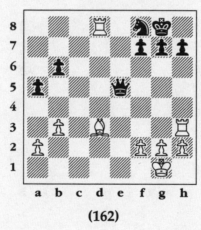

(162)

Answers

161: 1 Nxc7+ Rxc7 2 Rd8 mate

162: 1 Bxh7+ Kh8 2 Rxf8 mate

BACK ROW MATES IN TWO MOVES

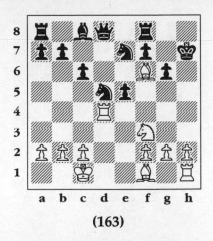

(163)

(164)

Answers

163: 1 Rh4+ Kg8 2 Rh8 mate

164: 1 Re8+ Nxe8 2 Rf8 mate

BACK ROW MATES IN TWO MOVES

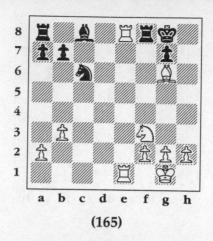

(165)

(166)

Answers

165: 1 Rxf8+ Kxf8 2 Re8 mate

166: 1 Qd8+ Bxd8 2 Re8 mate

BACK ROW MATES IN TWO MOVES

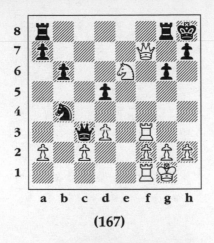

(167)

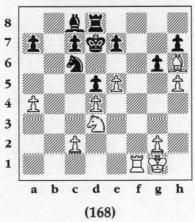

(168)

Answers

167: 1 Qxh7+ Kxh7 2 Rh3 mate

168: 1 Nc5+ Ke8 2 Rf8 mate

BACK ROW MATES IN TWO MOVES

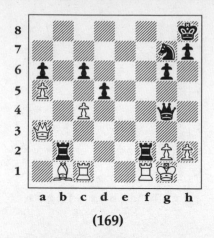

(169)

(170)

Answers

169: 1 Qf8+ Rxf8 2 Rxf8 mate

170: 1 Rxf8+ Qxf8 2 Qxf8 mate

BACK ROW MATES IN TWO MOVES

(171)

(172)

Answers

171: 1 Rxd8+ Rxd8 2 Qxd8 mate or 1 Qxd8+ Rxd8 2 Rxd8 mate

172: 1 Qb8+ Kxb8 2 Rxd8 mate

BACK ROW MATES IN TWO MOVES

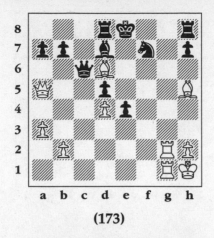

(173)

(174)

Answers

173: 1 Rg8+ Rxg8 2 Rxg8 mate

174: 1 Qxh7+ Kxh7 2 Rh3 mate

BACK ROW MATES IN TWO MOVES

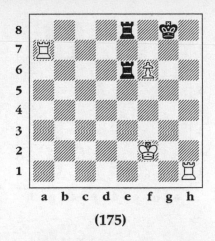

(175)

(176)

Answers

175: 1 Rg7+ Kf8 2 Rh8 mate

176: 1 fxg7+ Kg8 2 Rf8 mate

BACK ROW MATES IN TWO MOVES

(177)

(178)

Answers

177: 1 Qxf7+ Rxf7 2 Re8 mate or 1 Qxf7+ Kh8 2 Qxf8 mate

178: 1 Rxh7+ Kxh7 2 Qh5 mate

BACK ROW MATES IN TWO MOVES

(179)

(180)

Answers

179: 1 Qxh7+ Kxh7 2 Rh4 mate

180: 1 Qxh7+ Rxh7 2 Rg8 mate

BACK ROW MATES IN TWO MOVES

(181)

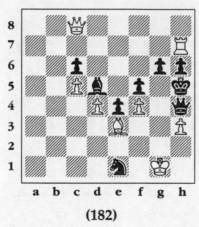

(182)

Answers

181: 1 Bh6+ Bg7 2 Qh8 mate or 1 Bh6+ Qg7 2 Qxh8 mate

182: 1 Rxh6+ Kxh6 2 Qh8 mate

BACK ROW MATES IN TWO MOVES

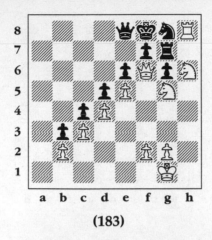

(183)

(184)

Answers

183: 1 Rxg8+ Rxg8 2 Nh7 mate or 1 Nh7+ Rxh7 2 Rxg8 mate

184: 1 Ng6+ hxg6 2 Qh3 mate

BACK ROW MATES IN TWO MOVES

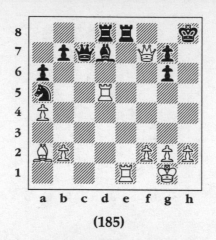

(185)

(186)

Answers

185: 1 Rh5+ gxh5 2 Qxh5 mate

186: 1 Qa8+ Rxa8 2 Rxa8 mate

BACK ROW MATES IN TWO MOVES

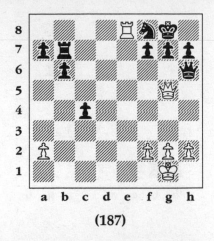

(187)

(188)

Answers

187: 1 Rxf8+ Kxf8 2 Qd8 mate

188: 1 Qg5+ Kf8 2 Qg8 mate or 1 Qxh7+! Kf8 2 Qg8 or
     Qxh8 mate or 1 Qxh7+! Kxf6 2 Qh6 mate!

BACK ROW MATES IN TWO MOVES

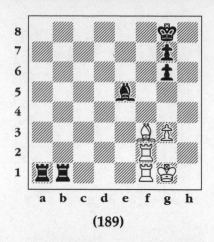

(189)

(190)

Answers

189: 1 Bd5+ Kh8 or Kh7 2 Rh2 mate

190: 1 Rh8+ Bxh8 2 Qxh8 mate

BACK ROW MATES IN TWO MOVES

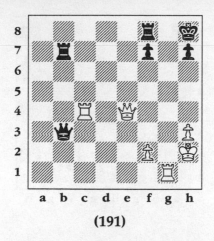

(191)

(192)

Answers

191: 1 Qxh7+ Kxh7 2 Rh4 mate

192: 1 Qxh6+ Kxh6 2 Rh8 mate or 1 Rh8+ Kxh8 2 Qxh6
mate

BACK ROW MATES IN TWO MOVES

(193)

(194)

Answers

193: 1 Ng6+ hxg6 2 Rh1 mate

194: 1 Qh5+ Kxh5 2 Rh7 mate

BACK ROW MATES IN TWO MOVES

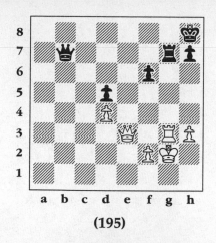

(195)

(196)

Answers

195: 1 Qe8+ Rg8 2 Qxg8 or Rxg8 mate

196: 1 Qf8+ Kh7 2 Qg7 or Rxh6 mate or 1 Qf8+ Bxf8 2 Rh8 mate

BACK ROW MATES IN TWO MOVES

(197)

(198)

Answers

197: 1 Ng5+ Kg8 or Kh8 2 Rd8 mate

198: 1 Nh6+ Kf8 2 Rg8 mate

BACK ROW MATES IN TWO MOVES

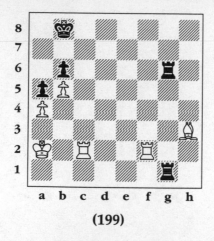

(199)

(200)

Answers

199: 1 Rc8+ Kb7 or Ka7 2 Rf7 mate

200: 1 Rb7+ Kc8 2 Ra8 mate

BACK ROW MATES IN TWO MOVES

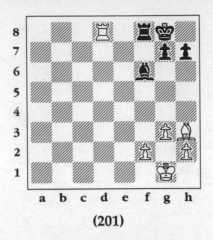

(201)

(202)

Answers

201: 1 Be6+ Kh8 2 Rxf8 mate

202: 1 Rh8+ Kxh8 2 Qxf8 mate

BACK ROW MATES IN TWO MOVES

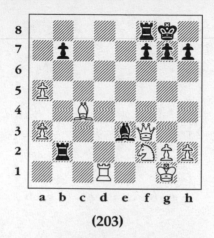

(203)

(204)

Answers

203: 1 Qxf7+ Kh8 2 Qxf8 mate or 1 Qxf7+ Rxf7 2 Rd8 mate

204: 1 Rxh7+ Rxh7 2 Qf8 mate

BACK ROW MATES IN TWO MOVES

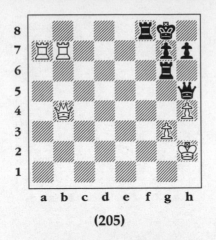

(205)

(206)

Answers

205: 1 Qxf8+ Kxf8 2 Ra8 or Rb8 mate

206: 1 Qe8+ Bf8 2 Qxf8 mate

BACK ROW MATES IN TWO MOVES

(207)

(208)

Answers

207: 1 Bc5+ followed by Re8 mate

208: 1 Bh6+ Kg8 2 Rxe8 mate

BACK ROW MATES IN TWO MOVES

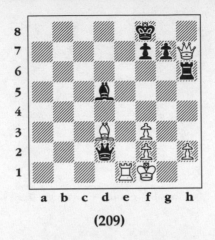

(209)

(210)

Answers

209: 1 Qg8+ Kxg8 2 Re8 mate

210: 1 Qe8+? Kh7 2 Rh1+ Rh5+!! but 1 Rh1+! Kg8 2 Qe8 mate!

BACK ROW MATES IN TWO MOVES

(211)

(212)

Answers

211: 1 Ng6+ Kg8 2 Rxf8 mate

212: 1 Be6+ Kf8 2 Rh8 mate

BACK ROW MATES IN TWO MOVES

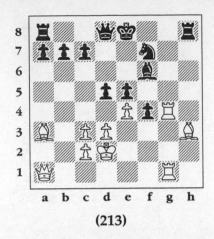

(213)

(214)

Answers

213: 1 Rg8+ Rxg8 2 Rxg8 mate

214: 1 Rg8+ Bf8 2 Rxf8 mate

BACK ROW MATES IN TWO MOVES

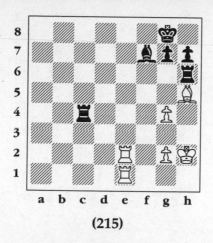

(215)

(216)

Answers

215: 1 Re8+ Bxe8 2 Rxe8 mate

216: 1 Qa8+ Qc8 2 Qxc8 mate

BACK ROW MATES IN TWO MOVES

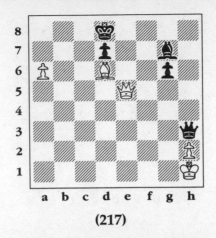

(217)

(218)

Answers

217: 1 Qe7+ Kc8 2 Qe8 mate

218: 1 Bxc6+ followed by Re8 mate

BACK ROW MATES IN TWO MOVES

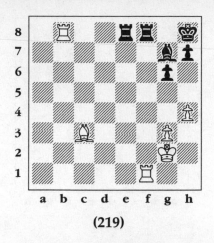

(219)

(220)

Answers

219: 1 Rxf8+ Rxf8 2 Rxf8 mate

220: 1 Qg8+ Rxg8 2 hxg8Q mate

BACK ROW MATES IN TWO MOVES

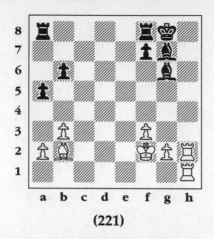

(221)

(222)

Answers

221: 1 Rh8+ Bxh8 2 Rxh8 mate

222: 1 Qh8+ Rxh8 2 Rxh8 mate

BACK ROW MATES IN TWO MOVES

(223)

(224)

Answers

223: 1 hxg6+ (double check!) Kg8 2 Rh8 mate

224: 1 Qc4+ Kh8 2 Qc8 mate

MORE CHECKMATES IN TWO MOVES

Positions 225-424 are all checkmates in two moves but they have been divided into groups to make it a little easier for you to know what to look for. The page headings will tell you what the groups are.

The first groups are checkmates by the different pieces. There are not very many queen checkmates because many of the rook and bishop checkmates could be made by the queen also.

Afterwards comes a group of checkmates by various pieces but in every case the victim is a black king that has castled. As your opponent will castle in most games you play, it is important to know the main ways of trying to checkmate him near the corner of the board. In many of the examples you will find that White's job has been made easier by the breaking up of the protecting wall of pawns in front of the black king.

The section of discovered and double checks includes some difficult positions. Do not worry if you cannot do them. Sometimes the double check is on the first move and sometimes it is the checkmate.

We finish with a group of all sorts of checkmates just to see if you are now beginning to spot the main types.

QUEEN MATES IN TWO MOVES

(225)

(226)

Answers

225: 1 Qh7+ Kf8 2 Qxf7 mate

226: 1 Ne7+ Kh8 2 Qxf8 mate

QUEEN MATES IN TWO MOVES

(227)

(228)

Answers

227: 1 Qd3+ Ke6 2 Qd7 mate

228: 1 Nfe7+ Rxe7 2 Qf8 mate or 1 Qg7+ Rxg7 2 Nh6 mate

QUEEN MATES IN TWO MOVES

(229)

(230)

Answers

229: 1 Ne6+ Ke8 2 Qd8 mate

230: 1 Bxe6+ followed by Qxh7 mate or 1 Bxh7+ Kh8 2 Nf7 mate

QUEEN MATES IN TWO MOVES

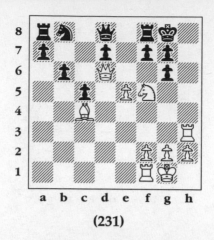

(231)

(232)

Answers

231: 1 Qxg6 followed by either Qxg7 or Qh7 mate

232: 1 Qh7+ Kf7 2 Qxg7 mate

130

QUEEN MATES IN TWO MOVES

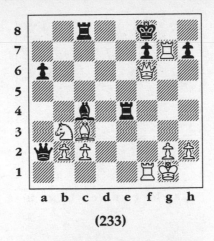

(233)

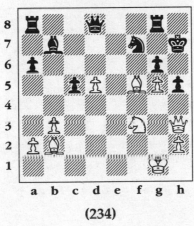

(234)

Answers

233: 1 Rg8+ Kxg8 2 Qg7 or Qh8 mate

234: 1 Qxh5+ Nh6 2 Qxh6 mate

QUEEN MATES IN TWO MOVES

(235)

(236)

Answers

235: 1 Rf7+ Kg8 2 Qe8 mate

236: 1 Rxg8+ Kxg8 2 Qe8 mate

ROOK MATES IN TWO MOVES

(237)

(238)

Answers

237: 1 Re8+ Rxe8 2 Rxe8 mate

238: 1 Rxh7+ Kg8 2 Rdg7 mate

ROOK MATES IN TWO MOVES

(239)

(240)

Answers

239: 1 hxg6+ (double check!) Kg7 2 Rh7 mate

240: 1 Ne7+ Kh8 2 Rxf8 mate

ROOK MATES IN TWO MOVES

(241)

(242)

Answers

241: 1 Bh7+ Kh8 2 Rxf8 mate

242: 1 Qxh6+ Qxh6 2 Rxg8 mate or 1 Qxh6+ Qh7 2 Qxh7 or Rxg8 mate

ROOK MATES IN TWO MOVES

(243)

(244)

Answers

243: 1 Bh6+ Kg8 2 Re8 mate

244: 1 Bf6+ Kg8 2 Rd8 mate

ROOK MATES IN TWO MOVES

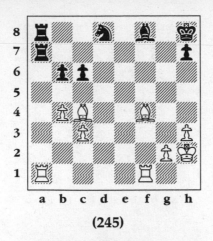

(245)

(246)

Answers

245: 1 Be5+ Bg7 2 Rf8 mate or 1 Be5+ Rg7 2 Rxf8 mate

246: 1 Nd7+ Ke8 2 Rg8 mate

ROOK MATES IN TWO MOVES

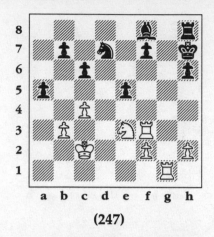

(247)

(248)

Answers

247: 1 Rxf7+ Bg7 2 either Rxg7 mate

248: 1 Nf6+ Bxf6 or Kf8 2 Re8 mate

ROOK MATES IN TWO MOVES

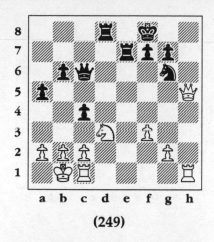

(249)

(250)

Answers

249: 1 Qh8+ Nxh8 2 Rxh8 mate

250: 1 Qxg8+ Kxg8 2 Rf8 mate

ROOK MATES IN TWO MOVES

(251)

(252)

Answers

251: 1 Qxa5+ Kb8 2 Rd8 mate

252: 1 Qxf7+ Rxf7 2 Rd8 mate or 1 Qxf7+ Kh8 2 Qxf8 mate

ROOK MATES IN TWO MOVES

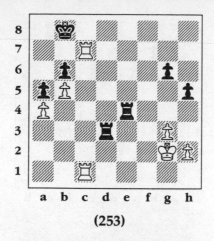

(253)

(254)

Answers

253: 1 Rc8+ Kb7 or Ka7 2 R1c7 mate

254: 1 Qxh7+ Kxh7 2 Rh3 mate

ROOK MATES IN TWO MOVES

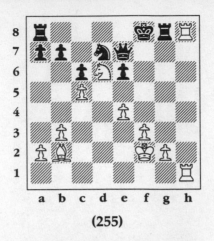

(255)

(256)

Answers

255: 1 Rxg8+ Kxg8 2 Rh8 mate

256: 1 Ba6+ Ka7 or Ka8 2 Bc8 mate

ROOK MATES IN TWO MOVES

(257)

(258)

Answers

257: 1 Rf8+ Rg8 2 either Rxg8 mate

258: 1 Rh8+ Kg5 2 Rh5 mate

ROOK MATES IN TWO MOVES

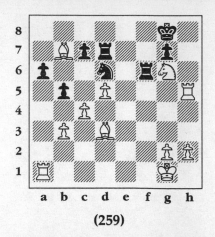

(259)

(260)

Answers

259: 1 Rh8+ Kf7 2 Rf8 mate

260: 1 Qxf8+! Qxf8 2 Rxh7 mate

144

ROOK MATES IN TWO MOVES

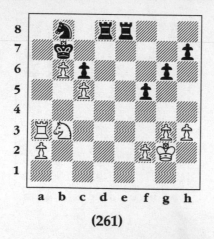

(261)

(262)

Answers

261: 1 Ra7+ Kc8 2 Rc7 mate

262: 1 Qxg7+ Rxg7 2 Rxg7 mate

ROOK MATES IN TWO MOVES

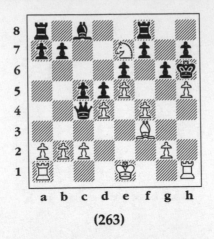

(263)

(264)

Answers

263: 1 hxg6+ Kg7 2 Rxh7 mate

264: 1 Rxh7+ Kg8 2 Rdg7 mate

ROOK MATES IN TWO MOVES

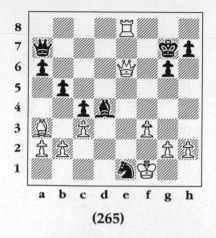

(265)

(266)

Answers

265: 1 Bf8+ Kh8 2 Bh6 mate

266: 1 Qf6+ Kf8 or Ke8 2 Rh8 mate

ROOK MATES IN TWO MOVES

(267)

(268)

Answers

267: 1 Nf5+ Kh5 2 Rg5 mate

268: 1 Rh1+ Bh2 2 Rxh2 mate

BISHOP MATES IN TWO MOVES

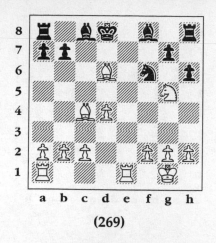

(269)

(270)

Answers

269: 1 Nf7+ Kd7 2 Bb5 mate

270: 1 Rd8+ Rg8 2 c4 mate

BISHOP MATES IN TWO MOVES

(271)

(272)

Answers

271: 1 Bf6+ Kf8 2 Nh7 mate or 1 Bf6+ Kg6 2 Bf7 mate

272: 1 Qxe6+ fxe6 2 Bg6 mate

BISHOP MATES IN TWO MOVES

(273)

(274)

Answers

273: 1 Bf5+ Kc7 2 Bd8 mate

274: 1 h6+ Kxh6 2 Bf8 mate

BISHOP MATES IN TWO MOVES

(275)

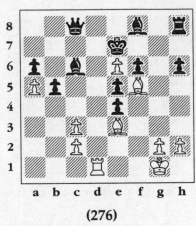

(276)

Answers

275: 1 Rf8+ Kg7 2 Bh6 mate

276: 1 Bc5+ Ke8 2 Bg6 mate

BISHOP MATES IN TWO MOVES

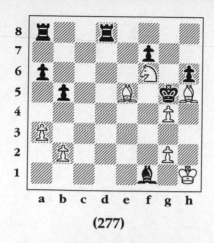

(277)

(278)

Answers

277: 1 Ne4+ Kh4 2 Bf6 or Bg3 mate

278: 1 Kf8 followed by Bc3 mate

BISHOP MATES IN TWO MOVES

(279)

(280)

Answers

279: 1 g4+ Kh4 2 Be1 mate

280: 1 Qxf7+ Rxf7 2 Bxf7 mate or 1 Bxf7+ Rxf7 2 Qxf7 mate

BISHOP MATES IN TWO MOVES

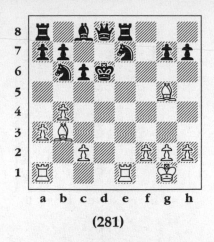

(281)

(282)

Answers

281: 1 Bf4+ Kd7 2 Be6 mate

282: 1 Qxg4+ Kxg4 2 Be2 mate

BISHOP MATES IN TWO MOVES

(283)

(284)

Answers

283: 1 Qxc6+ bxc6 2 Ba6 mate

284: 1 Bd5+ Ne6 2 Bxe6 mate or 1 Bd5+ Bxd5 2 Rf8 mate

KNIGHT MATES IN TWO MOVES

(285)

(286)

Answers

285: 1 Rf8+ Rxf8 2 Ng7 mate

286: 1 Rdxd8+ Qxd8 2 Ne7 mate

KNIGHT MATES IN TWO MOVES

(287)

(288)

Answers

287: 1 Qg8 + Rxg8 2 Nf7 mate

288: 1 Rxh6+ Kg8 2 Ne7 mate

KNIGHT MATES IN TWO MOVES

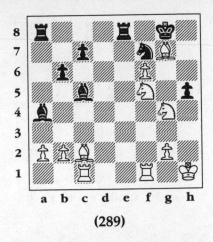

(289)

(290)

Answers

289: 1 Nfh6+ Nxh6 2 Nxh6 mate but not 1 Ngh6+? Kh7 2 Ne7+ Bxc2

290: 1 Qe7+ Kg8 2 Nh6 mate

KNIGHT MATES IN TWO MOVES

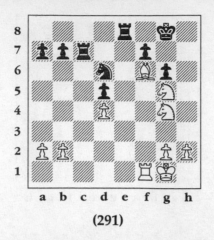

(291)

(292)

Answers

291: 1 Nh6+ Kf8 2 Nh7 mate

292: 1 Qh8+ Bxh8 2 Nh7 mate or 1 Ne6+ fxe6 2 Qxg7 mate

KNIGHT MATES IN TWO MOVES

(293)

(294)

Answers

293: 1 Rxf7+ Nxf7 2 Ng6 mate

294: 1 Qxh7+ Qxh7 2 Nf7 mate

KNIGHT MATES IN TWO MOVES

(295)

(296)

Answers

295: 1 either Ne6+ Nxe6 2 Nxe6 mate

296: 1 Ng7+ Kf4 2 Ne2 mate

PAWN MATES IN TWO MOVES

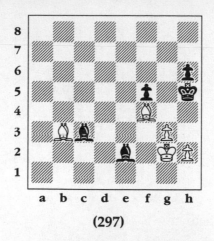

(297)

(298)

Answers

297: 1 Bf7+ Kg4 2 h3 mate

298: 1 Rxh7+ Kg5 2 h4 mate

PAWN MATES IN TWO MOVES

(299)

(300)

Answers

299: 1 Nh4+ Ke6 2 d5 mate

300: 1 d5+ cxd5 2 cxd5 mate

PAWN MATES IN TWO MOVES

(301)

(302)

Answers

301: 1 Bf7+ Nxf7 2 exf7 mate

302: 1 Qf7+ Rxf7 2 exf7 mate

PAWN MATES IN TWO MOVES

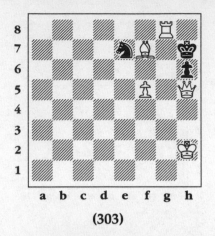

(303)

(304)

Answers

303: 1 Qg6+! Nxg6 2 fxg6 mate

304: 1 Bd5+ Nxd5 2 exd5 mate

PAWN MATES IN TWO MOVES

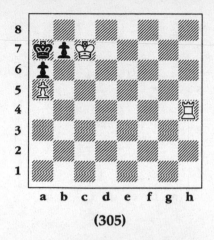

(305)

(306)

Answers

305: 1 Rh8! b6 2 axb6 mate or 1 Rh8! b5 2 axb6 en passant, mate

306: 1 Qxc3+ Nxc3 2 b4 mate

PAWN MATES IN TWO MOVES

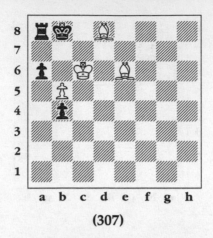

(307)

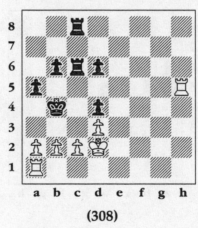

(308)

Answers

307: 1 Bc7+ Ka7 2 b6 mate

308: 1 a3+ Ka4 2 b3 mate

CHECKMATING THE CASTLED KING

(309)

(310)

Answers

309: 1 Rh8+ Kxh8 2 Qh7 mate or 1 Rh8+ Qxh8 2 Qf7 mate

310: 1 Bxa6 and mate next move by either Qc7 or Qd8 depending upon Black's move

CHECKMATING THE CASTLED KING

(311)

(312)

Answers

311: 1 Rxg7+ Kxg7 or Kh8 2 Qxh7 mate or 1 Qxh7+ Kf7 2
Qxg7 or Rxg7 mate

312: 1 Rg7+ Kxg7 2 Qh7 mate

CHECKMATING THE CASTLED KING

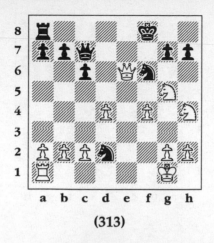

(313)

(314)

Answers

313: 1 Nxh7+ Nxh7 2 Ng6 mate

314: 1 Nxa7+ Kd7 2 Bb5 mate

CHECKMATING THE CASTLED KING

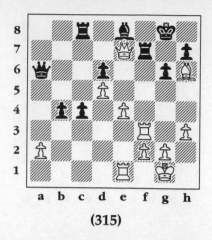

(315)

(316)

Answers

315: 1 Qf8+ Rxf8 2 Rxf8 mate

316: 1 Rb8+ Nxb8 2 Qb7 mate or 1 Rxc7+ and Qb7 mate

CHECKMATING THE CASTLED KING

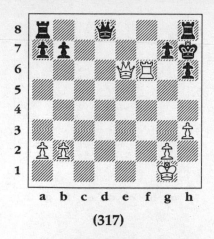

(317)

(318)

Answers

317: 1 Rxh6+ gxh6 2 Qf7 mate!

318: 1 Rxf7+ Kxf7 2 Qg7 mate

CHECKMATING THE CASTLED KING

(319)

(320)

Answers

319: 1 Rxb6+ Ka7 2 Qb7 mate or 1 Rxc7+ Kb8 2 Qb7 mate

320: 1 Qh7+ Kf8 2 Qg8 or Qh8 mate or 1 Qh7+ Kxf6 2 Qxh6 mate

CHECKMATING THE CASTLED KING

(321)

(322)

Answers

321: 1 Ng6+ hxg6 2 Qh3 mate

322: 1 Nd6+ either Nxd6 2 Qxb8 mate or 1 Nd6+ Qxd6 2
Qb7 mate

CHECKMATING THE CASTLED KING

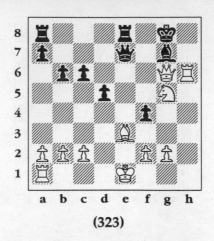

(323)

(324)

Answers

323: 1 Rh8+ Kxh8 2 Qh7 mate

324: 1 Qf8+ Bg8 2 Qxf6 mate

CHECKMATING THE CASTLED KING

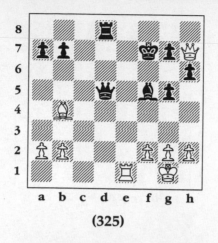

(325)

(326)

Answers

325: 1 Re7+ Kf8 or Kf6 2 Qxg7 mate

326: 1 Qh6! and Qg7 mate next move

CHECKMATING THE CASTLED KING

(327)

(328)

Answers

327: 1 Nf8+ (double check!) Kh8 or Kg8 2 Qh7 mate

328: 1 Rxd8+ Kxg7 2 Qg5 mate

CHECKMATING THE CASTLED KING

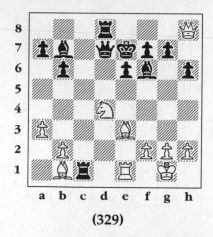

(329)

(330)

Answers

329: 1 Nf5+ exf5 2 Bc5 mate (double check!)

330: 1 Rh8+ Nxh8 2 Rxh8 mate

CHECKMATING THE CASTLED KING

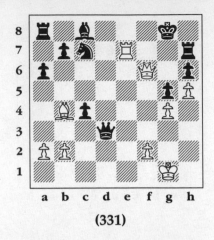

(331)

(332)

Answers

331: 1 Re8+ Nxe8 2 Qf8 mate

332: 1 Qxf7+ Kh8 2 Qxf8 mate or 1 Qxf7+ Rxf7 2 Rd8 mate

CHECKMATING THE CASTLED KING

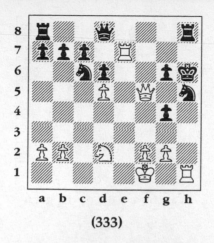

(333)

(334)

Answers

333: 1 Rxh5+ gxh5 2 Qf6 mate or 1 Qf4+ g5 2 Qf6 mate

334: 1 Rf8+ Kxf8 2 Qf7 mate

CHECKMATING THE CASTLED KING

(335)

(336)

Answers

335: 1 Qxf6+ either Rxf6 2 Rxh7 mate

336: 1 Rxh7+ Kxh7 2 Qh5 mate

DISCOVERED AND DOUBLE CHECKS

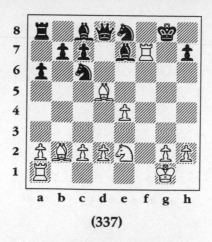

(337)

(338)

Answers

337: 1 Rg7+ Kh8 or Kf8 2 Rg8 mate

338: 1 Bc6+ Kf8 2 Re8 mate

DISCOVERED AND DOUBLE CHECKS

(339)

(340)

Answers

339: 1 Bd6+ Ke8 2 Rf8 mate

340: 1 Nd6+ Kd8 2 Qe8 mate

DISCOVERED AND DOUBLE CHECKS

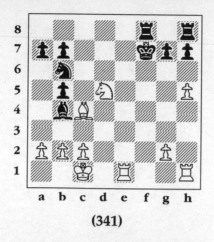

(341)

(342)

Answers

341: 1 Rhf1+ Kg8 2 Ne7 or Nf6 mate

342: 1 Nf6+ Kd8 2 Qe8 mate

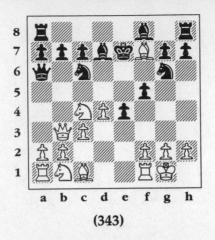

(343)

(344)

Answers

343: 1 Bg5+! Kxf7 2 Nd6 mate

344: 1 Rxh6+ Kxh6 2 Qg6 mate or 1 Rg8+ Rf5 2 Bxf5 or Qg6 mate

DISCOVERED AND DOUBLE CHECKS

(345)

(346)

Answers

345: 1 Nhg6+ Kg8 2 Rh8 mate or 1 Nxf5+ Kg8 2 Ne7 mate

346: 1 Rg5+! Rf7 2 Qxf7 mate or 1 Rg5+! Rxb3 or Bd5 2 Bxh7 mate or 1 Bxh7+ Qxh7 2 Rg5 mate! (double check)

DISCOVERED AND DOUBLE CHECKS

(347)

(348)

Answers

347: 1 Nb5+ Ka8 2 Ra7 mate

348: 1 Ng6+ hxg6 2 hxg3 mate!

DISCOVERED AND DOUBLE CHECKS

(349)

(350)

Answers

349: 1 Nd7+ Ka8 2 Nc7 mate

350: 1 Rh5+! Kg7 2 Rxg6!! mate

DISCOVERED AND DOUBLE CHECKS

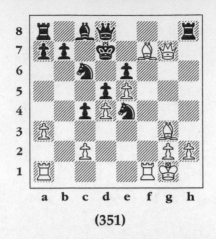

(351)

(352)

Answers

351: 1 Bxe6+ or Be8+ followed by Qf7 mate

352: 1 Rd6+ Rxd6 2 Ne6 mate

DISCOVERED AND DOUBLE CHECKS

(353)

(354)

Answers

353: 1 Nf8+ Kh8 2 Qh7 mate

354: 1 Re7+ Kh8 2 Rh7 mate

DISCOVERED AND DOUBLE CHECKS

(355)

(356)

Answers

355: 1 Re5+ Kd6 2 c5 mate!

356: 1 Nf5+! Ke8 2 Nxg7 mate

DISCOVERED AND DOUBLE CHECKS

(357)

(358)

Answers

357: 1 Nf6+ Kh8 2 Nf7 or Ng6 mate or 1 Nf6+ Kf8 2 Ng6
mate or 1 Ne7+ and Ng6 mate (which works even
without the second white knight)

358: 1 Nf5+ Kg8 2 Nh6 mate! or 2 Ne7 mate

DISCOVERED AND DOUBLE CHECKS

(359)

(360)

Answers

359: 1 Ng5+ hxg5 2 hxg6 mate

360: 1 Nxe6+ Kh7 or f4 2 Qxg7 mate or 1 Nxe6+ g5 2 hxg6 en passant mate!

...riest ...child in ...cked, while ...have a single ...t in their past will ...remain in ministry ...tain conditions.

...all of the conditions are ...ied, I'd be comfortable ...th allowing a priest to remain ...n ministry," said Bishop Martin Amos, who serves the southern region of the Roman Catholic Diocese of Cleveland, including Summit, Medina and Wayne counties.

"But I think it's going to be hard to fulfill all the criteria, and I don't see how any priest (with a single act of abuse) can go back into parish ministry. I think they will be OK in a more specialized ministry away from children."

The recommendation is part

Please see **Bishops, A7**

a (left),
with golf
old photo.

Today's Adver

(361)

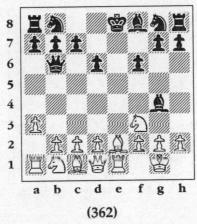

(362)

Answers

361: 1 Nf6+ Kf8 2 Qe8 mate or 2 Rd8 mate

362: 1 Bb5+ Kf7 2 Be8 mate or 1 Bb5+ Kd8 2 Re8 mate

DISCOVERED AND DOUBLE CHECKS

(363)

(364)

Answers

363: 1 Qg7+!! Bxg7 2 Nf6 mate

364: 1 Rxg7+ Kh8 2 Rxh7 or Rg8 mate or 1 Rxf8+ Kxf8 2
Qf7 mate

DISCOVERED AND DOUBLE CHECKS

(365)

(366)

Answers

365: 1 Nxd7+!! Qe7 2 Qxe7 mate or 1 Nxd7+!! Ne6 or Ne4 or Nxe2 2 Nf6 mate!!

366: 1 hxg5+ Kg8 or Kg6 2 Ne7 mate!!

DISCOVERED AND DOUBLE CHECKS

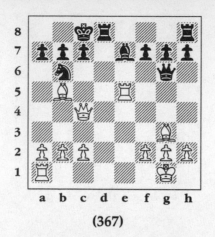

(367)

(368)

Answers

367: 1 Qxc7+ Kxc7 2 Rc5 mate

368: 1 Rg7+ Kh8 2 Rg8 mate

DISCOVERED AND DOUBLE CHECKS

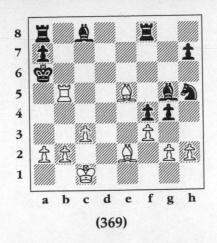

(369)

(370)

Answers

369: 1 Rb4+ Ka5 2 Bc7 mate

370: 1 Nf7+ Kg8 2 Nh6 mate

DISCOVERED AND DOUBLE CHECKS

(371)

(372)

Answers

371: 1 Bf6+ Kxf6 or Kh6 2 Qg5 mate

372: 1 Rg4+ Kh6 or Kh8 2 Nxf7 mate

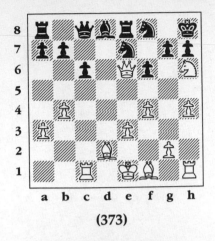

(373)

(374)

Answers

373: 1 Qg8+ Nxg8 2 Nf7 mate

374: 1 Qh7+ Kxh7 2 Bf7 mate

QUEEN SACRIFICES TO FORCE MATE

(375)

(376)

Answers

375: 1 Qe7+! Rxe7 2 Nf6 mate

376: 1 Qf7+! Nxf7 2 Ne6 mate

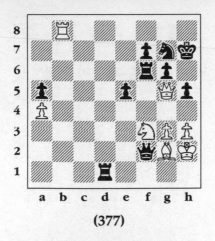

(377)

(378)

Answers

377: 1 Qh6+ Kxh6 2 Rh8 mate

378: 1 Qxc6+! Bxc6 2 Nxe6 mate

QUEEN SACRIFICES TO FORCE MATE

(379)

(380)

Answers

379: 1 Qc8+! Rxc8 2 Nd7 mate

380: 1 Qxc6+ bxc6 2 Ba6 mate

VARIOUS CHECKMATES IN TWO MOVES

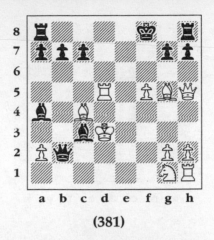

(381)

(382)

Answers

381: 1 Qf7+!! Kxf7 2 Rd8 mate!

382: 1 Nh5+ Ke8 2 Nxf6 mate or 1 Nh5+ Kg8 2 Qg5 mate

VARIOUS CHECKMATES IN TWO MOVES

(383)

(384)

Answers

383: 1 Nd7+ Bxd7 2 Rd5 mate

384: 1 Rxh7+ Kxh7 2 Rh1 mate

VARIOUS CHECKMATES IN TWO MOVES

(385)

(386)

Answers

385: 1 Rf5+ gxf5 2 Rg5 mate

386: 1 a7+ Kc8 2 a8Q or a8R mate

VARIOUS CHECKMATES IN TWO MOVES

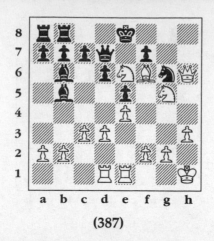

(387)

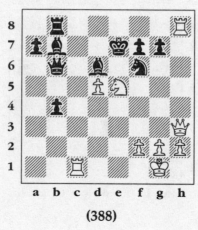

(388)

Answers

387: 1 Qf8+ Nxf8 2 Ng7 mate

388: 1 Ng6+ fxg6 2 Qe6 mate

VARIOUS CHECKMATES IN TWO MOVES

(389)

(390)

Answers

389: 1 Bc5+ Qxc5 2 Qd7 mate or Bc5+ Qd6 2 Qd7 mate

390: 1 h4+ Kg4 2 Rg6 mate

VARIOUS CHECKMATES IN TWO MOVES

(391)

(392)

Answers

391: 1 Bb8! followed by Nc7 mate or if 1 . . . b5 2 Nxc5 mate

392: 1 Ra5+ bxa5 2 b5 mate

VARIOUS CHECKMATES IN TWO MOVES

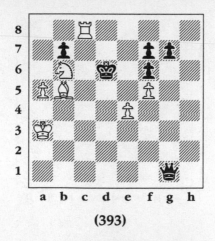

(393)

(394)

Answers

393: 1 Nc4+ Ke7 2 Re8 mate

394: 1 Ng6+ hxg6 2 Rh1 mate

VARIOUS CHECKMATES IN TWO MOVES

(395)

(396)

Answers

395: 1 Nd5+ Ke6 2 Nef4 mate

396: 1 Rf6+ Kxe5 2 Bf4 mate

VARIOUS CHECKMATES IN TWO MOVES

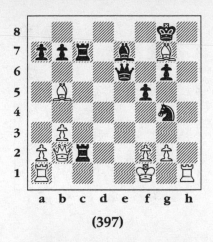

(397)

(398)

Answers

397: 1 Rh8+ Kf7 2 Be8 mate

398: 1 Bxg6+ Kxg6 2 Qh5 mate

VARIOUS CHECKMATES IN TWO MOVES

(399)

(400)

Answers

399: 1 Bf4+ gxf4 2 gxf4 mate

400: 1 Qe4+!! Kxe4 2 Nc3 mate or 1 Nc3+ Ne3 2 Qe4 mate

VARIOUS CHECKMATES IN TWO MOVES

(401)

(402)

Answers

401: 1 f5+ Kf7 2 Nd6 mate

402: 1 Nf7+ Kd7 2 Be6 mate

VARIOUS CHECKMATES IN TWO MOVES

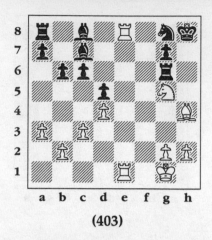

(403)

(404)

Answers

403: 1 Rxg8+ Kxg8 2 Re8 mate

404: 1 Reb7+ Kc5 2 Ra5 mate

VARIOUS CHECKMATES IN TWO MOVES

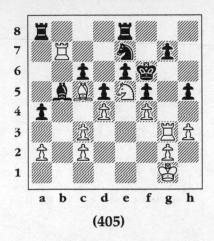

(405)

(406)

Answers

405: 1 Bxe7+ Rxe7 2 Rg6 mate or 1 Rg6+ Nxg6 2 Rf7 mate or 1 Rxe7 followed by either Rf7 mate or Rg6 mate or Nd7 mate depending upon Black's move.

406: 1 either Rf6+ Bxf6 2 Rxf6 mate

VARIOUS CHECKMATES IN TWO MOVES

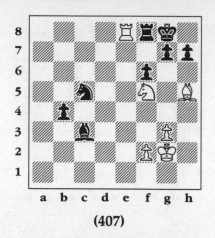

(407)

(408)

Answers

407: 1 Ne7+ Kh8 2 Rxf8 mate

408: 1 Rxh6+ Kxh6 2 Rh3 mate

VARIOUS CHECKMATES IN TWO MOVES

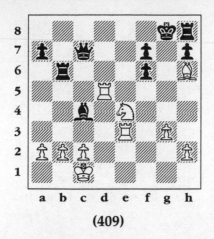

(409)

(410)

Answers

409: 1 Nxf6+ Rxf6 2 Re8 mate

410: 1 Rh4+ Nxh4 2 g4 mate but not 1 Rg5+?? Nxg5+!

VARIOUS CHECKMATES IN TWO MOVES

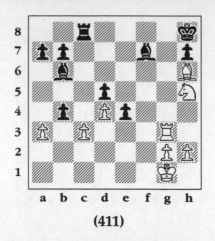

(411)

(412)

Answers

411: 1 Bg7+ Kg8 2 Nf6 mate

412: 1 Bxf7+ Kf8 2 Ng6 mate

VARIOUS CHECKMATES IN TWO MOVES

(413)

(414)

Answers

413: 1 Nd6 a1Q 2 Nf7 mate

414: 1 Re8+ Nxe8 2 Bh7 mate or 1 . . . Rf8 2 Rxf8 or gxf8Q
or gxf8R mate!

VARIOUS CHECKMATES IN TWO MOVES

(415)

(416)

Answers

415: 1 Nf5+ Kxh5 2 Rh2 mate or 1 Ng8+ Kxh5 2 Rh2 mate

416: 1 Bh3+ Kf4 2 Nf1 or Ne4 mate!

VARIOUS CHECKMATES IN TWO MOVES

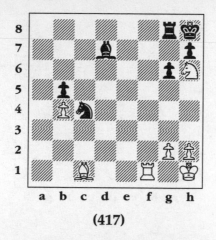

(417)

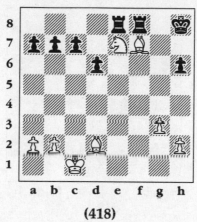

(418)

Answers

417: 1 Nf7+ Kg7 2 Bh6 mate

418: 1 Bc3+ Kh7 2 Bg6 mate

VARIOUS CHECKMATES IN TWO MOVES

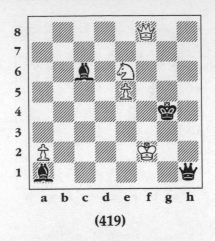

(419)

(420)

Answers

419: 1 Qf4+ Kh5 2 Qg5 mate or 1 Qf4+ Kh3 2 Qg3 or Ng5 mate

420: 1 Nf5+ Ke8 2 Nxg7 mate

VARIOUS CHECKMATES IN TWO MOVES

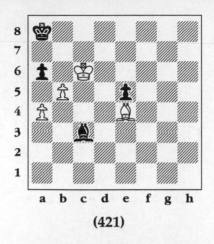

(421)

(422)

Answers

421: 1 Kc7+! Ka7 2 b6 mate

422: 1 Qxg7+ Bxg7 2 Nf6 mate

VARIOUS CHECKMATES IN TWO MOVES

(423)

(424)

Answers

423: 1 Ne6! g6 2 hxg6 mate or 1 Ne6! g5 2 hxg6 en passant, mate

424: 1 Kf8! followed by 2 Rh5 mate

SOME HARDER MATES IN TWO MOVES

Even when the answers are only two moves long, it is possible to have quite difficult positions and here we have three examples. If you wish, you can try them yourself before we discuss them. White to play and checkmate in two moves, as before.

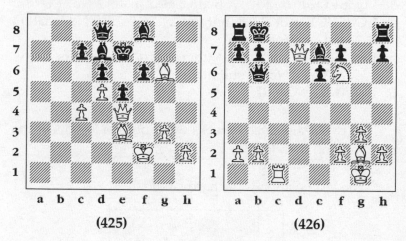

(425)   (426)

425: Notice that the black king cannot move and that neither the white queen nor the white bishop on e3 are doing anything, yet. If the bishop could go to either c5 or g5 with check it would be mate, so the queen has to sacrifice herself to make this possible.

1 Qxe5+!! fxe5 2 Bg5 mate or 1 . . . . dxe5 2 Bc5 mate or 1 . . . . Be6 2 Qxc6 mate. The difficulty of this position lies in the surprising first move for White. It is hard to even think about a move which means taking something protected by two pawns, especially when you are taking with your queen.

Position 426 is complicated because there are several possible answers and you need to discover which ones work and which fail. The basic idea is very simple; White is going to play Nd7 mate. At the moment his queen is in the way so White will obviously move her in order to threaten

227

the mate. He will move her with check so that Black does not have time to play something like a6 which makes it possible to get out of the mate (if Nd7+ then Ka7). There are 6 queen checks—which work?

1: 1 Qxb7+ Qxb7 2 Nd7+ Qxd7.
2: 1 Qc7+ Qxc7 2 Nd7+ Qxd7.
3: 1 Qd6+ Qxd6 (not 1 . . . . Bxd6 2 Nd7 mate) 2 Nd7+ Qxd7.
4: 1 Qd8+ Qxd8 or Rxd8 (but not 1 . . . . Bxd8 2 Nd7 mate) 2 Nxd7+ Q (or R) xd7.
5: 1 Qe8+ Rxe8 2 Nd7 mate! but what if 1 Qe8+Q (or B) to d8? Then 2 Nd7 is still mate!
6: 1 Qc8+ Rxc8 2 Nd7 mate!

So two of the queen checks work but the last one is the simplest and therefore the best.

The last position is the hardest of all.

(427)

Black threatens checkmate himself by Rh1 and there is no way for White to get out of this threat unless he can find a checkmate himself. First look at the checks by the white queen on f7, g8 and h8. You will quickly see that they lead to nothing except the loss of the queen. That leaves only the two bishop checks. Are they any good or is just one of them playable? If just one, which one?

1 Bh6+ Kxh6 2 Qh8 mate looks good but what if 1 Bh6+ Kh7! (chess players often refuse presents of that sort). Now White can only play 2 Qxf7+ Kxh6 3 Qf8+. Look at this position carefully. Black has to play Kh7 and White can again play Qf7+ when Black has to reply either Kh8 or Kh6 and in either case White plays Qf8+ again forcing the black king back to h7. Because White is going to lose immediately to Rh1 mate, he must continue to check the black king. The black king cannot get away from the checks and so we have a situation where White can check forever. This is called *perpetual check* and it is counted as a draw. This is an important way of saving a lost position—it is not unsporting play. What about the other bishop check? 1 Bf6+ Kh7 2 Qh8 mate or 1 Bf6+ Kxf6 2 Qh8 mate! Quite simple really provided you can work out that the last position is mate.

NOT ALWAYS CHECK

In working through the book you will have seen that we have included a few examples of mate in two where the first move was not a check but Black could still not avoid checkmate on the next move. Such examples are quite rare but it is interesting to look at the various ways in which it is possible to bring this about. The main ways to checkmate in two moves without a check on the first move, are:

1: play a move (usually with the checkmating piece) to threaten an unstoppable checkmate.
2: play a move to stop the king's only move so that you can checkmate next move.
3: play a move to threaten two (or more) checkmates where Black cannot stop them all.
4: where you are already threatening a checkmate, capture the piece that is defending against it.

5: you play a move so that Black's only legal move is one which allows you to checkmate.
6: a special type of number one is the case of a pawn promoting leaving a position where Black cannot avoid checkmate from the new piece.

On pages 231 to 233 you will find one example of each type but not in the same order.

THE FIRST MOVE IS NOT CHECK

(428)

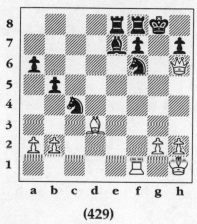

(429)

Answers

428: 1 b8Q Ka1 2 Qb2 mate or 1 b8Q Ka3 2 Qb3 mate. Move the two kings up and down the files to see when a mate in two is possible. There is a position when promotion to a rook works.

429: 1 Rxf6 and there is no way to prevent Qxh7 mate next move.

THE FIRST MOVE IS NOT CHECK

(430)

(431)

Answers

430: 1 Qe4! (threatens Qe8 mate and Qxh7 mate). Black cannot prevent both.

431: 1 Rh6! c4 (the only legal move) 2 Rf5 mate.

THE FIRST MOVE IS NOT CHECK

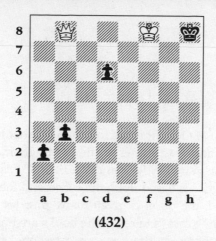

(432)

(433)

Answers

432: 1 Qe8! and Qh5 mate next move. If Qa7, Qb7 or Qc7 then a1Q prevents an immediate checkmate. All other queen moves are answered by Kh7.

433: 1 Bf5! traps the king so that White may play either Ne6 mate or Ne4 mate next move.

Among the other positions in this book you will find further examples of most of these six types.

ABOUT THE AUTHOR

TONY GILLAM taught chess to primary school children (age 7-9) and was trainer to the Nottingham Primary Schools team in the 1960s and 1970s. His "Discovering Chess" series is based upon the successful methods he developed: the pupil is given many puzzles to solve, with no long essays to read. The books are highly suitable for young children, yet are presented in such a way as to be appropriate for novices of all ages.

He has been involved in chess publishing for many years. His company, The Chess Player, has published many books on specialist aspects of chess, including opening monographs and historical texts. He has edited more than 300 chess books, including the flagship periodical, *The Chess Player*, which provided coverage of international chess from 1971 to 1980.